Everyday

CHRISTIAN

A USER'S GUIDE

TOM BRUBAKER

Copyright © 2025 Tom Brubaker All rights reserved.

No part of this publication may be reproduced, stored, or transmitted in any form or by any means, including written, copied, or electronically, without prior written permission from the author or his agents. The only exception is brief quotations in printed reviews. Short excerpts may be used with the publisher's or author's expressed written permission.

All Scripture quotations, unless otherwise noted, are from the Revised Standard Version of the Bible.

26.2: Occasional Marathoner, Everyday Christian

A User's Guide

Cover and Interior Page design by True Potential, Inc.

ISBN: (Paperback): 9781960024657

ISBN: (e-book): 9781960024664

LCCN: 2025902123

True Potential, Inc.
PO Box 904, Travelers Rest, SC 29690
www.truepotentialmedia.com
Produced and Printed in the United States of America.

"By weaving appropriate Bible Scriptures into preparing for, training for and running a marathon race, Tom offers readers a unique, helpful and valuable insight into what it takes and means to be a Christian. He makes it clear that a life lived in faith is surely a marathon and to be true to it takes a long term approach. Therefore I highly recommend this book to believers and non-believers alike!"

Christopher Hart. Host of The American Adversaries Radio Show and Podcast and Author of Politics and *Pro-Wrestling How to Understand and Cope with the Mayhem*

"As a former 30 year smoker and non-runner, I managed to log 10 marathons and too many half marathons to count. Divine intervention had to have prevailed. But the inspiration for me to run my first 5K goes to the author. It all started there and then the Good Lord provided the path. A great read that will inspire many to commit to a run with Christ."

- Jim Schauble, Tom's co-runner for 20+ years

"Tom Brubaker's book, **26.2: Occasional Marathoner, Everyday Christian***, serves as a helpful and extremely practical book on running, faith, and life. This book serves as a daily "check-in," chalk full of motivational tips and tricks on how to grow as a runner, as a Christian, and as a person. If you are looking for something that's easy to read, enjoyable, encouraging, and able to share with others, I highly recommend this resource!"*

Drew Taylor. Willow Creek Church Associate Pastor of Connections & Discipleship

"Tom Brubaker describes himself as a middle-of-the-pack runner - and Christian - but this is no ordinary book. At a time when many people get turned off by Christian leaders who crave the attention of the front row or who teach that there's only one way to run, Brubaker shows us that the marathon of faith is an extraordinary journey made up of ordinary steps and you can make your way to the finish line using many training methods and running styles.

26.2: Occasional Marathoner, Everyday Christian is a training manual for those who have the humility to run their race from the middle, where you never know what sorts of people you will meet and where cheering on or simply keeping pace with our fellow runners can be a means of everyday grace - much like this book.

Dr. Glenn Whitehouse. Professor of Philosophy & Religion Florida Gulf Coast University

Contents

Preface	7
Disclaimer	11
Part 1: Deciding to Race	**13**
1. All Types of People Enter the Race	17
2. Running a Marathon Is Difficult	23
3. Running a Marathon Requires the Right Mindset	29
4. Encountering Doubters, Naysayers, and Hecklers	35
5. You Will Learn More About Yourself	43
Part 2: Preparing to Race	**49**
6. Find the Right Race Location	51
7. Training Methods Can Vary	57
8. Find a Support System	63
9. Outfit Yourself for the Race	69
10. Proper Nutrition Is Important	75
11. Start Small and Give Yourself Time to Improve	79
Part 3: Running the Race	**83**
12. Pick Up Your Race Packet	85
13. Show Up the Morning of the Race	91
14. Find the Right Starting Corral	95

15. The First Mile is Always the Slowest	101
16. Count the Mile Markers	105
17. Expect the Lonely Stretches	111
18. Cliché, But True: Blood, Sweat, and Tears	117
Part 4: Finishing the Race	**123**
19. Hitting the Wall	125
20. Music Helps	131
21. Spectators Can Give You a Boost	137
22. Water Stops Can Be Lifesavers	143
23. Don't Neglect the Last 0.2 Mile	147
24. Cross the Finish Line Proudly	153
Part 5: Beyond the Finish Line	**159**
25. Stick Around for Post-Race Activities	161
26. Display Your Medal	167
Afterword	171
26.2 You Don't Know Who You May Inspire	173
Tom's Marathons	176
About the Author	177

Preface

The idea for this book came to me around mile six of the Garden of Life Marathon (West Palm Beach, Florida) on December 10, 2023.

My daughter had signed up for her first full marathon, and she convinced me to run it as well. Having completed nine full marathons before, I was no stranger to the training such a race requires.

Unfortunately, I did not train enough. From the start of the race, I knew I would be lucky just to finish. By mile six, I began to doubt whether I could even "gut it out," as I had in previous marathons.

Let me explain something: I run, but I do not consider myself a Runner. To me, being a Runner is a lifestyle—subscribing to magazines devoted to running, following industry trends, adopting the latest running technology, and otherwise immersing oneself in the world of running. There's nothing wrong with that, and I respect the industries that support it, but that's just not me.

So why do I run? I usually deflect the question with answers like, "I love a challenge," "I want to see what I'm made of," or "I'm trying to lose weight." My goal for any marathon is simply to finish the race—to survive running 26.2 miles. (The only exception was in 2006, when I aimed to break the four-hour mark—and succeeded.)

The truth is, I run marathons because they require me to focus, both physically and mentally, on a specific task. I consider myself a middle-of-the-pack marathoner—an average guy who finishes somewhere in the middle of the overall group of runners.

That morning in West Palm Beach, I tried to distract myself from the increasing pain by comparing the challenge of running 26.2 miles to the challenges of being a Christian. I don't know where the idea came from; it just popped into my head. My wife and I had recently joined a church, rekindling my relationship with God and my interest in Christianity. As I ran, I began thinking of 26 ways running this race was akin to being a Christian.

The pain eventually became unbearable, and I tapped out at the halfway point. But the idea for this book stayed with me. Some of the analogies in this book may fall short, so please remember that I'm just an average guy who runs unimpressive marathons and lives what I consider a middle-of-the-pack Christian lifestyle.

If you are considering either challenge—running a marathon or following Christ—I hope you find some wisdom in these pages. If you've already taken up either challenge, I hope this book offers you fresh perspectives on what you've accomplished and where you're headed.

By the way, my daughter finished her first marathon quite strong.

Disclaimer

Regarding Running

- I am not a coach.
- I am not a trainer.
- I am not an expert.

I know what works for me, and I train for my marathons accordingly. If you plan to run, seek out a proper training regimen or consult a professional.

Regarding Christianity

- I am not ordained.
- I have not studied philosophy.
- I am not a leader in my church.

I'm just an ordinary, average guy who considers himself a middle-of-the-pack Christian. I've attended and been a member of various Protestant denominations, including Presbyterian, Methodist, Baptist, and the Christian Church. Currently, I'm a member of Willow Creek Church (Presbyterian Church in America) in Winter Springs, Florida.

The purpose of this book is to offer personal reflections while remaining relatively neutral. I acknowledge that my opinions lean toward a Protestant perspective, but I hope to resonate with people from all walks of life—non-Christians, new Christians, and established Christians alike.

Part 1: Deciding to Race

"Now bid me run, and I will strive with things impossible."

~ William Shakespeare; spoken by Caius Ligarius; *Julius Caesar*, Act II, Scene I

Why start the book with a quote from a murderous conspirator? Ligarius had doubts about the plot against Caesar, but Brutus eased his doubts and assured him that their actions were honorable. Ligarius accepted the rationale and followed Brutus's bidding into murder.

Running a marathon and following God are certainly not assassination plots, but like Ligarius, you may wrestle with doubts about the decision. So, my question is: What bids you to run?

Reasons for deciding are varied, ranging from overwhelming inspiration…

- **Physically** – Perhaps you are inspired by someone living a healthy lifestyle, and you want to do the same.
- **Emotionally** – Perhaps life is good, but you want to take on new challenges.
- **Spiritually** – Perhaps God has made Himself known to you, and you want to respond to His call.

…to overwhelming desperation…

- **Physically** – Perhaps you are sick and tired of how you look or feel, and you know you must do something to change.
- **Emotionally** – Perhaps life has bottomed out, you don't see any purpose, and you need something—anything—to keep going.
- **Spiritually** – Perhaps you recognize a spiritual emptiness within yourself, but you know someone who professes the Christian faith, and you want to experience the same.

…or something in between…

- **Physically** – Perhaps you live a healthy lifestyle but want to take it to a new level.
- **Emotionally** – Perhaps you've hit a rough patch in life and are compelled to make some changes to get things back on track.
- **Spiritually** – Perhaps you grew up in a Christian home or are already a believer, but you're ready to engage at a deeper level.

…but you are certain of one thing: You want to make the commitment!

If you are considering either choice, reflect on the circumstances I just described. If you've already made the decision, think back to what your situation was when you made it.

This portion of the book covers the aspects leading up to signing on the dotted line.

OBSERVATION #1

ALL TYPES OF PEOPLE ENTER THE RACE

My first observation may sound simplistic, even obvious, but I bring it to your attention because it's an essential part of your decision to enter:

Not everyone who runs a marathon is a world-class athlete.

In addition to marathons, I've run road races of various distances, such as 5K (3.1 miles), 10K (6.2 miles), and half-marathons (13.1 miles). At all of these events, I've seen participants of every kind:

- Short and tall runners
- Young and old runners

26.2

- Fast and slow runners
- Husky and thin runners
- Runners who run with a partner, a group, or solo
- Runners who listen to music and those who don't
- Runners who high-five every spectator they see and those who keep to themselves
- Runners with two legs, runners with prosthetic legs, and wheelchair participants
- Conversationalists who talk throughout the race and quiet loners who are serious and focused in their strides
- Runners of all backgrounds—Black, white, Hispanic, Asian, and others

The same applies to the various churches I've attended. Correlating with the types of runners I just described, you'll find people from every walk of life in church:

- People who are outgoing and those who keep to themselves
- People who sing during worship and those who worship silently
- People who bow their heads during prayers and those who look around
- Worshipers who lift their hands during the service and those who don't
- Single people, married couples, young families, solo parents, and multi-generational families
- Men who wear a coat and tie every Sunday and those who wear Hawaiian shirts and jeans

Occasional Marathoner, Everyday Christian

There's nothing wrong with the people listed here. Everyone in the first list is at least running the race. Everyone in the second list is at least attending church.

At both a race event and in church, you'll find people who are either very similar to you or vastly different in terms of personality, mannerisms, and habits. Recognize that you're in the same place together, so you have that in common. Others may be seeking something different from what you're seeking, but you're both in the same place to find it.

As you approach your decision to enter the race, remember that your reasons may not align with everyone else's—and that's okay. Don't fall prey to rationalizations that could prevent you from committing, such as:

- "I'm not in shape."
- "I'm not a runner."
- "It's too much work."
- "This isn't my style."
- "I won't be able to keep up."
- "I don't want to deal with new people."
- "I can't make this sort of commitment."
- "I have better things to do with my time."
- "I don't want people looking at me."
- "I'm different from everyone else; I won't fit in."
- "Runners/churchgoers are weirdos."

Deciding to run can be exciting, scary, or even a welcome relief. However you feel about it, realize that many others

26.2

have made—or are in the process of making—the same decision. Most people are different from you, but some may be quite similar.

All types of people enter the race. Count yourself among them.

Reflection Point

"I can do all things in him who strengthens me."

Philippians 4:13

The Apostle Paul was in prison when he wrote these words. In his letter, he assured the church at Philippi (whose members were persecuted for their faith) that he had the strength to endure because his strength came through his faith in Christ.

Reflecting on your decision to enter the race, think about your reasons for wanting to start, and answer the following questions:

1. If you are already a Christian, what was your life like at the time you knew you wanted to follow God? If you are not yet a Christian, what might be a reason to choose to follow God?

26.2

2. What doubts and fears pull at you that may discourage you from "signing up" for the race?

3. If you are already a Christian, are you able to find strength through Christ the way Paul claimed he did? If you are not yet a Christian, what gives you spiritual strength?

OBSERVATION #2

Running a Marathon Is Difficult

I was overly anxious to run my first half-marathon. "13.1 miles—how hard can it be?" I thought. But my brother talked some sense into me. He explained that I didn't fully understand what running 13.1 miles was really like, and he convinced me to sign up for the accompanying 5K run instead. I am so glad I took his advice.

That first 5K was an eye-opener. I had "trained" by running one or two miles whenever I could find the time. I mapped out a training route, ran at an easy pace, and never overexerted myself. I thought I had it in the bag.

During that first race, I was surrounded by hundreds of other entrants, and I couldn't help but notice their forms and styles. I began to second-guess myself. Was my stride wrong? Was I wearing the right shoes and clothing? And the noise! Hundreds upon hundreds of running shoes pounding the street sounded like a muffled stampede.

Previously, I had watched plenty of races my brother ran, but I was always stationed near the finish line, where the runners were significantly spaced apart. Now, I was in the thick of it, having barely crossed the starting line, feeling out of place. I consciously stopped comparing my running style to others. I found my pace and finished the 5K feeling good about myself. In other words, I ran my own race.

I was sore for several days afterward. My brother's warning about the half-marathon made sense, and I couldn't even fathom running a full marathon.

If you have trouble appreciating what 26.2 miles feels like, try a simple exercise. The next time you're on a road trip driving on the interstate, set your car's trip meter to zero at a recognizable landmark, and then note the point where you reach 26 miles.

Now imagine running that distance.

There is nothing easy about running a marathon—nothing. You must recognize it for what it is, or you risk being overwhelmed by the experience. But running a marathon is completely doable. Almost every week, somewhere in America (usually on Sunday mornings), people embrace this difficult task and achieve what they may have once thought impossible. They run 26.2 miles, collect a medal for finishing, and prove that it's not impossible.

If you've chosen to enter a marathon, I'd love to tell you that the hardest part is over. But it's not. It doesn't get easier, either.

So, if it's so hard, why do it?

The answer is surprisingly simple, and you can probably guess it. The satisfaction of completing a marathon is unlike anything you'll ever know. It's not necessarily better than other life experiences, but it's something you achieve solely through your own hard work and commitment. Nobody else can run those miles for you.

Similarly, every week in America on Sunday morning, something else happens: People attend church—perhaps for the first time, perhaps for the first time in a long while, or perhaps as regular attendees. Some new churchgoers may feel out of place, just as I did during that first 5K.

When you choose to follow Christ, you go to Him and tell Him you're ready. He will give you your own race to run. Of course, there will be others in the race with you, and you may look to them for guidance and inspiration, but your race is unique. Find your pace and run your own race.

If you've chosen to become a Christian, I'd love to tell you that the hardest part is over. But it's not. It doesn't get easier, either.

Abiding by Christ's teachings means rising above the inclinations of human nature. It means facing a world filled with temptations that defy the Lord's teachings. That's tough.

So, if it's so hard, why do it?

26.2

Like a marathon, there's immense personal satisfaction in knowing you're upholding the life God calls you to live. Satisfaction does not mean vanity. Being a Christian doesn't make you better than anyone else. Being a Christian means you are a humble servant who consciously chooses to walk God's path. In return, He grants you peace and eternal life.

The primary reason for being a Christian is that it's what God calls us to do. We exist to honor and glorify God. It really is that simple. In giving you your own race to run, He will not call you to do anything you cannot handle. It may not be easy, but it is certainly doable.

Running a marathon is difficult, but take heart—you have tools, methods, and resources to assist you as you embark upon your race. It will most definitely hurt at times, and there are many miles ahead.

Reflection Point

Enter by the narrow gate; for the gate is wide and the way is easy, that leads to destruction, and those who enter it are many. For the gate is narrow and the way is hard, that leads to life, and those who find it are few.

Matthew 7:13-14

In this passage, Jesus acknowledges that following Him (by entering through the narrow gate) is a difficult path. The normal ways of the world (accessed through the wide gate) are easy, but they lead to destruction and ruin.

Christ never said that following Him would be easy. But, as with running a marathon, the satisfaction you receive for finishing is indescribable.

Reflecting on the acknowledged difficulty of the race, think about times in your life when you faced difficult

26.2

choices, and answer the following question:

1. Have you ever fully followed through on a resolution (New Year's resolution or otherwise)? If so, what drove your commitment to follow through? If not, what circumstances prevented you from following through?
2. What are some reasons people might fear committing to Christ?
3. What has been the most difficult decision you have made in life up to this point? What was at stake? What were the results (good or bad)?

OBSERVATION #3

RUNNING A MARATHON REQUIRES THE RIGHT MINDSET

Registering for a marathon is a commitment. At the bare minimum, you must pay the entry fee. After that, you're under no obligation to run the race. In fact, you're under no obligation to train or even have anything else to do with the race. You paid the money, so you can boast that you signed up for a marathon!

There is always a percentage of entrants who do not show up on race day. To be fair, some no-shows are due to unforeseen or unavoidable circumstances (medical, family, travel). But other no-shows happen because the entrants did not fully commit to running the race.

26.2

If you sign up for a race, you intend to run it—but you may not be fully committed to running it. Commitment requires you to put some skin in the game.

Entrants typically register for a marathon months in advance. This allows time to train for the race. Training marks a mindset shift from intention to commitment. Commitment involves action and investment (of both time and money); in other words, skin in the game. Such action and investment require much from you, including, but not limited to:

- Performing training runs
- Buying suitable clothing and equipment
- Increasing mileage on training runs
- Not quitting when the training starts to hurt
- Showing up at the starting line on race day

I have trained for marathons on a shoestring budget, wearing cheap running clothes and clearance-priced shoes. I have completed training runs in the rain, wind, cold weather, and on hot, muggy days. I continued training despite leg cramps, shin splints, and foot blisters. But I always maintained the mindset that I was going to show up on race day.

With regard to being a Christian:

At what point does your mindset shift from intention to commitment? How do you put skin in the game as a Christian? What actions and investments are required to participate in this race?

There are many possible answers to these questions, but here are three basic ones to consider as starting points:

1. Pray

Your commitment to the Lord is personal, so incorporate prayer into your daily routine. Think of this as your daily training run. If prayer is new to you, keep it short and simple. Ask for guidance. Thank Him for helping you through the day. Seek forgiveness for a wrongdoing. Thank Him before a meal. Just talk with Him daily.

2. Attend church

Committing to the Lord means exposing yourself to His Word, preferably through an ordained pastor. I'll discuss finding a church that fits your style in another chapter, but aim to attend (or tune in online) once a week and absorb the message.

3. Give

Yes, I'm talking about money. This is often a touchy topic, but it's important. Churches operate in the real world, and that includes bills, salaries, and other expenses.

Like marathon training runs, start small—give enough that you notice it, but not so much that it causes hardship. If you truly cannot give financially, give your time by volunteering or serving in an outreach program. Your time is valuable, and offering it in His service is meaningful.

Committing to run a marathon is a (temporary) lifestyle change. Training requires more than daily exercise; you are building yourself up to accomplish an incredible feat. Success demands the right mindset.

Committing to live as a Christian is also a lifestyle change. This doesn't mean spending every moment of every day in reflection and prayer. It doesn't mean severing ties with all your friends to have only "church friends." It doesn't mean giving up all the creature comforts of modern life. What it does mean is maintaining a mindset of upholding the Lord as you navigate and serve Him in a challenging world.

With the proper mindset, you can accomplish what may currently feel impossible.

REFLECTION POINT

Do not be conformed to this world, but be transformed by the renewal of your mind, that you may prove what is the will of God, what is good and acceptable and perfect.

Romans 12:2

The Apostle Paul wrote the Book of Romans (in the form of letters) to the early church in Rome to instruct, encourage, and guide that society of Christians. This passage underscores the importance of this chapter's observation. To succeed amid persecution and hardship, those early Christians had to maintain the proper mindset. They had to put skin in the game.

There are times in life when we move from intent to commitment. Examples include:

- Getting married

26.2

- Having (or adopting) children
- Accepting a new job
- Moving to a different home
- Signing up for the Armed Forces

Reflect on times in your life when true commitment was required, and answer the following questions:

1. Does moving from intention to commitment need to be difficult?
2. Does moving from intention to commitment change who you are?
3. What do you give up when you move from intention to commitment? What do you gain?

OBSERVATION #4

ENCOUNTERING DOUBTERS, NAYSAYERS, AND HECKLERS

Unless you are the most private and solitary person imaginable, it is nearly impossible to keep a marathon a secret. You are going to tell someone, it will slip out, or someone will guess what you're doing. For the sake of argument, let's assume people know you've signed up to run a marathon.

In my experience, friends and family are mostly supportive. Sometimes they are cautious or guarded, and sometimes they poke a little well-intentioned fun. Occasionally, they are flat-out amazed, almost to the point of disbelief.

Not everyone is supportive, however. Intentionally or

unintentionally, someone can derail your marathon plans with a single comment.

As a Christian, you will face resistance as well. The world is full of people either opposed to or indifferent about Christianity. Often, these people (and organizations) are quite vocal; other times, they are deceptively subtle. You encounter them in everyday life as friends, family, acquaintances, coworkers, or complete strangers. You often hear from them through media channels, such as news outlets, radio, television, movies, and social media.

I categorize these individuals into three groups: **doubters**, **naysayers**, and **hecklers**.

Marathon Doubters

Marathon doubters are the people who directly doubt you and your ability to complete a marathon. They may comment on your health, lack of physical ability, or mental resolve. They may remind you of goals you've attempted but failed to achieve. They may even try to talk you out of it (thinking they're doing so for your own good). Doubters doubt you.

I am not a confrontational person. I often can't find the right words quickly enough to rebut a doubter. But at this point in my marathon journey, I have confidence in myself. I've thought through the decision to register. I've considered the potential negatives and what it will take to overcome them. I know my physical condition, and I'm aware that I won't set the world on fire with my race time.

I handle doubters by not engaging with them. I listen to their comments in case they say something worth considering. I nod and smile. I thank them for their concern. But I don't let them sway me. I've paid my entry fee and signed on the dotted line, so I'm committed to running the race.

I do not doubt my ability to run the marathon.

Christian Doubters

Christian doubters question your belief in Christ or your ability to maintain your faith. They may remind you of beliefs you once held but no longer do. They may ask if God could truly forgive your past actions. They may accuse you of turning to Christ as a crutch during a period of weakness or despair, claiming you'll abandon your faith when life improves.

Doubters may not bombard you with aggressive tirades. Instead, they might approach you with calm conversations as a friend, coworker, or family member. But recognize it for what it is—they doubt you and assume your faith will fade.

I deal with Christian doubters much like I deal with marathon doubters. I know what's in my heart and head. Becoming a Christian was a serious decision, and I am resolute. A doubter's words may sting (such as referencing painful moments from my past), but I maintain my composure and try to end the discussion diplomatically.

I do not doubt my belief in Christ.

Marathon Naysayers

Marathon naysayers are apathetic toward marathons in general. They're less direct than doubters, but their comments can still wear you down. They gripe about the race location and weather (too hilly, too hot). They ask why you pay so much money for a finisher's medal. They complain about how road races disrupt local traffic or share horror stories of people who've collapsed during a marathon. Naysayers are unsympathetic.

I handle naysayers similarly to doubters. I listen to their complaints but offer little rebuttal, knowing my decision is final.

But I might double-check the weather forecast for the race.

Christian Naysayers

Christian naysayers are generally neutral. They may accept your decision to follow Christ but have no desire to do so themselves. Perhaps life has been so smooth or rough that they see no reason to worship God. Maybe no one has introduced them to the Christian faith, so they don't hold it in high regard. Whatever the reasons, their attitude is often, "Good for you, but not for me."

My conversations with Christian naysayers are typically brief, usually ending with a polite "You go your way, and I'll go mine." While churches encourage members to reach out to nonbelievers, I find it easier to invite people to social church events, such as Easter egg hunts or fall festivals, than to regular services.

Naysayers don't rattle me. If the opportunity arises, I may ask why they're uninterested in Christianity and consider their answer. Otherwise, we part on speaking terms.

Marathon Hecklers

Marathon hecklers are mostly harmless but can still get under your skin. They actively comment on your running—sometimes jokingly, sometimes maliciously.

Hecklers might shout, "Run, Forrest!" while you're training. I've had firecrackers thrown at me from a car and encountered a vicious dog whose owner scolded me for running in the first place.

There are also unintentional hecklers. Some sit along race routes drinking beer and teasing runners to join them. Others offer cash to runners to quit. You've probably seen a "0.0: I Don't Run" sticker on someone's car. While often humorous, such remarks might demoralize a runner struggling through the last miles.

Hecklers are easy to handle. I smile, wave, or offer a wearied "Thanks!" and keep running.

Christian Hecklers

Unlike marathon hecklers, who are usually joking, Christian hecklers often cast serious aspersions. They might claim man created God, not the other way around. They might call Christians "mindless sheep" or accuse churches of indoctrination.

I frequently encounter Christian hecklers on social media, in interviews with public figures, or overheard workplace conversations.

As a middle-of-the-pack Christian, I don't have many Bible verses memorized, so I'm not equipped to counter hecklers with scripture. I endure the verbal attacks and rest firmly in my beliefs.

Reflection Point

Now when Sanballat heard that we were building the wall, he was angry and greatly enraged, and he ridiculed the Jews. And he said in the presence of his brethren and of the army of Samaria, "What are these feeble Jews doing? Will they restore things? Will they sacrifice? Will they finish up in a day? Will they revive the stones out of the heaps of rubbish, and burned ones at that?"

Nehemiah 4:6-3

The Book of Nehemiah recounts the rebuilding of Jerusalem's walls after the Babylonian conquest. Despite opposition, Nehemiah resisted taunts and threats, completing the seemingly impossible task in 52 days.

Reflecting on Nehemiah's story, think about a time in your life when you faced doubters, naysayers, or hecklers—whether against you personally or a group you were part of.

Answer the following questions:

1. What was the reason for this behavior?

2. What was the outcome of the situation? Were there any additional consequences?

3. Is it important to address doubters, naysayers, and hecklers? Why or why not?

OBSERVATION #5

You Will Learn More About Yourself

I have always been a procrastinator. I rationalize that while I'm not performing a task that must be done, I'm thinking about how I'm going to do it. I suppose that's true sometimes, but usually, this approach is exactly what I've labeled it: rationalization. However, if I'm going to run a marathon, I absolutely, positively cannot procrastinate.

When preparing for a marathon, I follow a training system that requires shorter daily runs during the workweek, with long runs on the weekends. I train in the early morning, long before anyone else in the house is awake (even the pets). I convince myself to get out of bed, put on my running clothes, stretch, and start my planned run.

There are times when I literally argue with myself to stay in bed. Only through sheer willpower do I get up and hit the road. During weekend distance runs, my thoughts often turn to questioning why I'm doing this. Why can't I find a different hobby? I usually satisfy myself by remembering the reasons I signed up for the race, which helps me grind out the training miles.

This is how I've come to know myself better. I, the procrastinator, can discipline myself to follow a routine in order to achieve a goal. I cannot skimp on the required miles. So I find myself running in the dark early morning, running in the rain, even running along roads where I risk being clipped by a passing car. I have a race to finish, and I must train for it.

Being a Christian requires willpower too.

When you accept Christ, you don't give up your free will. God allows you to make your own decisions and behave as you choose. His intent is that your thoughts and actions will glorify Him, but the decision is yours to make.

Some Sunday mornings, I find my bed quite comfortable, and I think that maybe God won't mind if I skip church this week.

In fairness, there are times when you're unable to go to church. Personal matters, such as illness, vacations, and other real-world commitments, sometimes prevent you from doing things you would normally do to glorify Him. That's OK—it really is. But as a Christian, you should remain aware of such missed opportunities. Don't allow one or two weeks of missing church to spiral into rationalizations like those I've mentioned. It's an easy habit to fall into.

It's easy to skip a training run and sleep in. It's easy to convince myself that I only need to run 10 miles this weekend instead of the 15 miles I had planned. But it's difficult (and miserable) to make up those missed miles. I've learned what it takes to overcome my procrastination in order to achieve my goal.

Do you know yourself well enough to put in the miles?

Reflection Point

Examine yourselves, to see whether you are holding to your faith. Test yourselves. Do you not realize that Jesus Christ is in you? — unless indeed you fail to meet the test! I hope you will find out that we have not failed.

2 Corinthians 13:5-6

In this letter to the church in Corinth, Paul reminded the followers that, as Christians, they were to exemplify Christ. As such, they should look inward to see how they were modeling that behavior. Were they putting on airs, or were they truly changed people who walked the walk?

Reflecting on this passage, look inward to examine yourself and answer the following questions:

1. What personal traits might impact your resolution to hold onto your faith?

2. How can you test yourself to determine how well you uphold your faith?
3. What do you hope to learn about yourself as you exercise your Christian faith? If you have been a Christian for some time, what have you learned about yourself as a result of your faith?

Part 2: Preparing to Race

"Give me six hours to chop down a tree, and I will spend the first four sharpening the axe."

~ Abraham Lincoln

You've made your decision: you're going to run. Now it's time to prepare for the marathon, starting with finding the right race location, registering for the race, and conditioning yourself for the task ahead. A marathon is about more than endurance; it requires both your body and your mind to finish the race, so you should prepare accordingly.

These analogies illustrate your journey as a Christian as well. It can be exciting when you first choose to follow Christ, but patience and preparation are required. The paradox of being a Christian is that it's incredibly simple, yet sometimes overwhelmingly complex. It's simple because all that's required is that you accept Christ. That's it. The complexity comes with how different denominations interpret the Word of God and the seemingly endless questions Christians ask about their own faith.

It takes time and faith to seek out the answers, so prepare yourself for the task ahead.

This portion of the book covers aspects to consider as you prepare for the race.

Get ready.

Observation #6

Find the Right Race Location

As if running 26.2 miles wasn't enough to worry about, choosing which marathon to enter is an important consideration. These races come in every possible configuration: large or small, road-based or trail-based, hilly or flat, daytime or nighttime, and more.

Marathons are often destination events; the organizers aim to attract participants from outside the area, supporting the local economy. If the marathon you plan to run is local, you won't need to worry about travel, lodging, or other associated costs. But if you have a destination race in mind, be prepared for those expenses.

You might see the term **fast-and-flat** associated with a marathon. This means the race route has minimal hills or inclines, resulting in faster finish times for most entrants.

26.2

You might see the term **Boston Qualifier** associated with a marathon. These are marathons in which completing the race within a certain time, based on gender and age group, qualifies you to enter the Boston Marathon.

You might see the term **field size** associated with a marathon. This refers to how many entrants can register for the race. Some marathons are huge events with thousands of runners. Larger, more popular marathons often manage registration through a lottery, leaving your entry to chance. Smaller marathons may host anywhere from fewer than 100 to maybe 1,000 runners.

Some marathons attract not only entrants but also local residents who come out to cheer the runners. I ran the Chicago Marathon in 2005 and the Marine Corps Marathon (Washington, DC) in 2006, and parts of those routes were packed with enthusiastic onlookers.

Other marathons are isolated events. I ran the Tobacco Road Marathon (Raleigh, NC) in 2011, much of which followed a trail through a state park. Aside from other runners and the folks manning the aid stations, there was hardly anyone around for much of the race.

Review what each location offers and find a race that works for you. For instance, if you want a marathon with huge crowds but find the course too hilly, you might want to keep looking.

As a Christian, selecting a church is similar to selecting a marathon.

There are several branches of Christianity, such as Catholicism, Protestantism, and Anglicanism. These branches

(Protestantism in particular) contain multiple denominations, such as Baptists, Methodists, and Presbyterians. A denomination may also contain multiple branches; for example, Methodism includes the United Methodist Church, the Free Methodist Church, the Wesleyan Church, and the Christian Methodist Episcopal Church.

Some churches take a very strict interpretation of Scripture, while others interpret the Bible more loosely.

Some churches sing only traditional hymns during services, while others perform contemporary Christian music. Some even worship without musical instruments.

Some churches hold a single weekly service, while others offer multiple services throughout the week or emphasize small group meetings among members.

I can't say that one type of church is better than another. As a middle-of-the-pack Christian, I don't know enough about different denominations to make a valid comparison. My point is that when you choose to live as a Christian, it helps to find a church that suits your style. This is where you will receive God's Word from your pastor, priest, minister, or whatever title the leader holds. This is where you will make a joyful noise in worship to Him.

When it comes to running a marathon, find a race that works for you. My preference is a fast, flat course, preferably close to home. I'm not picky about field size.

When it comes to living as a Christian, find a church that works for you. I grew up attending a Methodist church. As life rolled on, I attended other Protestant churches of various denominations that worked well for me because

26.2

they taught the Bible in ways relevant to modern life, and their congregations were friendly and welcoming.

Only you can decide which church works best for you, but make the decision thoughtfully and prayerfully. Ask questions and determine what a church's doctrine is. Does it truly align with what the Bible teaches? If you're new to the faith, you may not know enough to make that determination, but find out all you can.

Be patient and diligent. Finding the right fit may take time.

Reflection Point

"O come, let us worship and bow down, let us kneel before the Lord, our Maker!"

Psalm 95:6

King David is thought to be the author of Psalm 95. In this excerpt, he concisely captures the intent of worship. While there are passages throughout the Bible that speak of joyful noises, singing, and praise to the Lord, this verse reminds us that during worship, we should acknowledge the Lord as our Creator and remain humble and penitent before Him.

Reflecting on David's words and the observations in this chapter, think about your current situation. Whether you currently attend church or have not yet found one, answer the following questions:

1. What are the three most important features of a church to you?

26.2

2. If you currently attend a specific local church, how did you find it? If you don't currently attend a local church, how are you searching for one? Why or why not?

3. Do you consider remote church attendance (such as an online meeting space or televangelism) akin to attending a local church?

OBSERVATION #7

Training Methods Can Vary

When taking on something new, there often seems to be a pattern: hitting it hard, keeping at it for a while, but then tapering off—or stopping altogether. Gyms make fortunes from this behavior, especially around the New Year.

Perhaps you once wanted to learn to play a musical instrument, but now your guitar sits in a corner collecting dust, or your piano doubles as a bookshelf. Maybe your New Year's resolution to get in shape resulted in a treadmill that now serves as a laundry drying rack.

When training for a marathon, you won't start by running ten miles on your first training run. You must pace yourself and condition your body. I've followed different training methods leading up to my marathons, and they've worked fine for me. Search online, and you'll find dozens of training programs developed by specialists. Find one that suits your style and schedule.

The training models I use require short daily runs during the week and a longer-distance run once per week. Recovery days are part of the weekly schedule. As training progresses and the marathon date approaches, the distances for both daily runs and weekly long runs gradually increase.

The training method you choose explains what you need to do to prepare for your race. How you choose to train depends on your self-discipline. If you're focused and driven, you can train on your own. If you need accountability, want to share the experience, or simply enjoy company while running, train with someone else or join a group.

Find a program that makes sense to you and hold yourself accountable. Put in the miles and condition yourself. It may seem interminable, even tedious, but the payoff is worth it.

Consider a similar approach to practicing your Christian faith.

Attending church requires discipline. Reading your Bible or working through a Bible study program requires discipline. Attending small group studies requires discipline. Praying daily requires discipline. Volunteering your time requires discipline.

As with marathon training, find the right program you can commit to. Look for opportunities within your church that suit you. Join a small group or Bible study program. Find an outreach ministry where you can assist. Volunteer as a greeter. You may even identify a new need and start a ministry or outreach program.

Outside of church, look for opportunities to serve and demonstrate the goodness of the Lord. Walk in a charity event. Volunteer at a Christian-based organization. Deliver meals to shut-ins. Assemble meal packages for third-world countries.

The bottom line is that if you're living a Christian life, you should do what you can to glorify God and exemplify Christ. The payoff for putting in the effort is worth it.

Reflection Point

"A man without self-control is like a city broken into and left without walls."

Proverbs 25:28

This passage from Solomon describes the importance of guarding yourself against temptation and impulsive behavior. Without self-discipline, your plans may fall apart.

Many times during marathon training, I'm tempted to sleep in and skip a daily run. I can come up with half a dozen rationalizations for why I don't need to run today. But if I didn't exert the discipline to get out of bed and hit the road, I never would have run my first marathon—much less my ninth.

If you're a churchgoer, it's sometimes tempting to sleep in and skip church, isn't it? You might tell yourself, "It's only once," or, "I haven't missed a service in months," or,

"I've earned a week off." But the discipline required to walk the walk and live as a Christian helps keep temptations and secular attitudes in check, making your life as a Christian easier and more meaningful.

Reflecting on the need for discipline and self-control to achieve your goals in life, answer the following questions:

1. What events in your life required the most self-discipline, and what was the outcome of those events?

2. In the Biblical passage provided, what do you think is meant by "a city broken into and left without walls"?

3. In which areas would you be most likely to "stick to it" regarding serving in your church or in a Christian-based organization?

OBSERVATION #8

FIND A SUPPORT SYSTEM

I need a cheerleader every now and then when I'm training for a marathon. An occasional *attaboy* or *I'm proud of you* really goes a long way to boost my morale, especially as I get older and the miles become harder. I'll even take a compliment ending with *for a guy your age.*

I'm blessed to have a great family. My first wife, my current wife, my kids, and my extended family always have something good to say when they know I'm training for a big race.

Most of my training and distance runs are solo endeavors, but I've trained with a group for weekend long runs. Although I never became personally close with any of the group members, there was a camaraderie during those runs. There really is strength in numbers, and the miles often seemed easier when I was with that group.

If someone in the group was having a rough run, someone else would fall back, check in to make sure everything was OK, and adjust their pace to stay with the person having a hard time. There was no rule requiring this; it was simply a matter of supporting someone who was struggling.

Most midsize to large marathons feature pace groups. The leader of each group runs the marathon at a specific pace, such as 12 minutes per mile. The pace group leader usually carries a pole or sign that denotes the planned pace, and entrants run with that group accordingly, sticking together throughout the race.

During the seemingly endless miles of training runs, you may become discouraged and wonder why you're running at all. You may just want to throw in the towel and stop.

Support helps.

The same principles apply to living as a Christian. Christians don't seek praise or adulation. Christians live to glorify God, not themselves. It's humbling, and it can be downright discouraging at times, especially when you're going through a rough patch in life. But hearing an occasional *attaboy/attagirl* or *I'm proud of you* can help.

Not everyone is blessed with family or friends who share the same Christian values, but those who are have a great support system. That support can and should be reciprocal.

Your most obvious support system is your local church, where you participate in worship, fellowship, and ministry. There truly is strength in numbers here as well. If you're going through a tough time, seek support from like-minded friends and family. And if you encounter someone who's struggling, fall back, make sure everything is OK, and adjust your pace to support them.

Support helps.

Reflection Point

And let us consider how to stir up one another to love and good works, not neglecting to meet together, as is the habit of some, but encouraging one another, and all the more as you see the Day drawing near.

Hebrews 10:24-25

It's unclear who wrote the book of Hebrews, though it is often attributed to the Apostle Paul. The author channels Christ's instructions that we should encourage other believers as well as allow ourselves to be encouraged. We all need encouragement at some point.

Christianity is not a faith to be lived solo. Encouraging others and being encouraged is central to our lives as followers of Christ.

Many of the "big names" in the Bible had support systems. Consider Moses: he set the Hebrews free from slavery in Egypt and led them to the Promised Land, but he couldn't do it all by himself. His support system included his brother Aaron and his nephew Hur. Even the great ones need support.

Reflecting on the benefits of encouragement, answer the following questions:

1. Whether you are a new Christian, an experienced Christian, or not yet a Christian, think of a time when someone encouraged you in your beliefs. What was the motivation for the person offering encouragement?

2. What are some strategies for encouraging a person spiritually?

3. If you are a churchgoer, how does your church encourage its members? If you are not a churchgoer, how do you think a church should offer encouragement to its members?

OBSERVATION #9

OUTFIT YOURSELF FOR THE RACE

I've seen people wear some pretty wild outfits while running a marathon, ranging from tuxedos to superhero costumes, but those are exceptions. There are specially designed clothes for running, and you're going to spend some money to properly outfit yourself for the race.

Good running shorts are designed to be breathable and comfortable. Some shorts have pockets to store keys, a phone, or specially designed water bottles.

Most running shirts (and sports bras) are made from specialty materials designed to wick moisture away from your skin and keep you cool. I live in humid Central Florida, so no matter what shirt I wear, I'm sweat-soaked just a few miles into my run. Choose a comfortable size to minimize chafing.

Hats, sunglasses, visors, sweatbands, and other accessories are optional. There are also products designed to minimize chafing and protect the more sensitive areas of your body.

In my opinion, the most important gear is your shoes and socks. Long miles can lead to blistered feet and toes. Improper foot support can result in sore feet, shin splints, or a dozen other problems. If possible, visit a running store or sporting goods shop where they can assess your running style and outfit you appropriately.

When running a marathon, clothes truly do make the man (or woman).

Clothing in a Spiritual Context

Clothing is referenced throughout the Bible, from Genesis (where clothing was used to hide Adam and Eve's shame) to Revelation (with allusions to being clothed in fine linen).

Clothing often symbolizes righteousness. Just as running clothes provide comfort and protection, the robes of righteousness mentioned in the Bible comfort you in your choice to live a Christian lifestyle. They help protect you from the temptations and evils of the world. The robes of righteousness represent the virtue you receive when you choose to follow Christ.

Growing up, my parents had me wear my "Sunday best" when attending church, intending that I present my best self before the Lord. Many churches now have a relaxed dress code, and opinions on this vary widely.

Clothing is a representation of your personality and attitudes. Your clothing and outward appearance provide first impressions, and you're often judged (whether you like it or not) by how you dress and present yourself.

However you choose to dress for the Lord, both literally and figuratively, dress appropriately, and remember that you are dressing for His glory and honor, not your own.

Reflection Point

"Put on the whole armor of God, that you may be able to stand against the wiles of the devil."

Ephesians 6:11

This passage may sound familiar, as it is an oft-quoted portion of Scripture. In his letter to the Ephesians, Paul likens the virtues Christians should adopt (truth, righteousness, peace, faith, and salvation) to armor that helps you stand against the evils of the world. Think of it the same way you think of running clothes and equipment that protect you from the environment and the rigors of running.

Reflecting on this passage, answer the following questions:

1. How do the virtues implied in this passage provide protection from the evils of the world?

2. Which do you seek more from your righteous clothing: comfort or protection?
3. Do you ever find yourself making assumptions, speculations, or judgments based on another person's clothing?

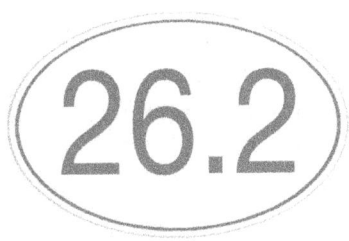

OBSERVATION #10

Proper Nutrition Is Important

When training for a marathon, proper nutrition has always been an afterthought for me. I don't count calories, fat grams, or carbohydrates. I don't follow special diets. I barely understand the science of nutrition. However, I try to be mindful of what I eat while training. I know not to eat a fast-food combo meal the night before a distance run. I know to "carb up" the night before a race by eating a meal like pasta to provide my body with energy during the run.

I'm a middle-of-the-pack marathoner. I have no illusions of placing in my age group, so I'm not going to drastically modify my eating habits while training. I'm mindful of what I eat, but I don't make it central to my running.

26.2

I admit that if I were to make the effort to follow a careful diet, my running would benefit. But it seems so difficult, expensive, inconvenient, and time-consuming.

Likewise, I know what proper spiritual nutrition should be—becoming inherently familiar with my Bible. Knowing at least the major sections and stories would be a good start. Reading a little bit of the Bible every day would be good sustenance for my spiritual well-being. Committing Bible verses to memory would be like "carbing up" before a big race.

Not knowing the Bible backward and forward doesn't make you a bad Christian, but it would benefit you to read it more often than just on Sunday mornings.

If you consider yourself a middle-of-the-pack Christian like me, there are other ways to get your spiritual nutrition. Join a Bible study group at your church. Find online resources or apps dedicated to Bible study. If you find the Bible boring or confusing, check out Christian study guides that help interpret the more challenging parts of Scripture.

Maintaining a spiritual diet is as challenging as maintaining a nutritional diet, but it's doable. You just have to carve out the time in your busy day. Read your Bible for five minutes over breakfast, during your lunch break, or right before bedtime. Although doctors may discourage you from consuming anything right before bedtime, ignore that advice and consume a little bit of His word before your head hits the pillow.

Reflection Point

"But he answered, 'It is written, 'Man shall not live by bread alone, but by every word that proceeds from the mouth of God.'"

Matthew 4:4

Jesus spoke these words when Satan tried to tempt Him in the wilderness. In these words, Jesus references Moses' statement to the Hebrews that God provided manna during their time in the desert. Physical nourishment is provided by God for those who believe and trust in Him, but spiritual nourishment is just as important.

Reflecting on both the physical and spiritual need for sustenance, answer the following questions:

1. What sort of "spiritual diet" do you follow (or would like to follow) to sustain your faith?

26.2

2. Some churches use food-based ministries (such as meal delivery programs and soup kitchens) as outreach opportunities. What are your thoughts on such programs?

3. In what ways can you incorporate prayer into your daily routine?

OBSERVATION #11

Start Small and Give Yourself Time to Improve

During one of my early Disney Marathons, a DJ stationed along the course stood on a high platform, blasting upbeat music, clapping oversized Mickey Mouse hands, and shouting encouragement to the runners. One of the things he said stuck with me: "This is where all of your training pays off!" He couldn't have been more correct.

Marathon training is a long-term commitment because you have to start small and gradually build up your mileage. That's a lot of running. It totals hundreds of miles, the last 26.2 of which make up the marathon itself.

Weekday runs start at one mile, three or four times per week. After a couple of weeks, the distance increases to

26.2

two miles. Then two miles increase to three miles, and so on, until weekday runs cap at seven miles.

Weekend distance runs require a similar buildup. My first long run might be three miles, some of which I walk. The following week, I increase to four miles. The pattern continues as dictated by my training plan. Before too long, I'm running in the double digits (10 miles or more).

Likewise, being a Christian is a long-term commitment. New Christians may approach spiritual growth similarly to marathon training: start small and increase over time.

If you don't have a Bible, purchase one in a version you can understand. Or ask your church to provide you with one that matches the version used in worship.

For your daily runs, start by reading your Bible for five minutes a day. Work to increase your time to ten minutes. Find a daily devotional to follow and increase your exposure to His word.

For your distance runs (which don't need to be limited to weekends), look for opportunities to serve or become more involved in your church. Join a small group if your church offers one. Attend a Sunday School class or Bible study session. Volunteer as a greeter or usher. Participate in outreach ministries or charitable programs.

As my mileage increases when training for a marathon, I feel the improvement, both physically and mentally. Similarly, as you increase your spiritual mileage, you'll feel improvement in your heart and soul. Start small and give yourself time to grow.

Reflection Point

"Practice these duties, devote yourself to them, so that all may see your progress."

1 Timothy 4:15

In this context, Paul wrote to his protégé Timothy, whom he sent to Ephesus to grow the Church and combat false doctrines. Paul, who was aging, knew that Timothy, though young and gifted, still had room to grow. Paul encouraged Timothy to stick to his principles and duties, knowing that growth would come through devotion and practice.

Regarding your spiritual growth, this passage simply advises you to stick to it. Just as starting small in marathon training strengthens your body and mind, starting small in spiritual practice strengthens your faith and heart, allowing you to grow. Paul reminds us that progress will come if we abide by the principles of our faith.

26.2

Reflecting on this point, consider your spiritual journey and answer the following questions:

1. Where do you consider yourself in terms of spiritual mileage? How did you get to where you are, and how do you plan to increase your mileage?
2. How might you develop a long-term strategy for spiritual growth?
3. What programs does your church offer that you might consider participating in?

Part 3: Running the Race

I'll be there someday, I can go the distance. I will find my way if I can be strong. I know every mile will be worth my while. When I go the distance, I'll be right where I belong.

~ Hercules, Walt Disney Company, *Hercules*

It's time. You've conditioned yourself and worked hard. There may have been missteps, even a few stumbles, but you're ready to toe the starting line. If this is your first time, your goal is likely just to go the distance. Even if you're experienced, your goal may still be to just go the distance. As a middle-of-the-pack kind of guy, I don't run marathons regularly, so my goal is almost always to just finish the race.

If you've studied, trained, and prepared properly, you should have a good idea of what to expect out on the course. If you've run warm-up races (such as 5Ks, 10Ks, or half-marathons) leading up to this one, you should have a sense of what the overall event will be like.

My experience after running nine of these monsters is that I often underestimate what 26.2 miles will demand of me. Each marathon is a new experience.

Even if you're physically prepared, remember that running a marathon is a mental task too. Approach it accordingly:

- You may want to think of your marathon in terms of time: *I just need to keep pace for four or five hours.*
- You may think of it in terms of distance: *Every mile behind me is one mile closer to the finish line.*

Running the Christian race also involves tasks, rituals, and sacraments that you've learned about and prepared to partake in. Actually crossing the starting line, however, requires serious self-reflection and mental preparedness.

Despite what many people in today's world may say, Christianity is not a cult. You don't sign your life away or give up all worldly possessions to abide by Christ's teachings. However, if you intend to cross that starting line to follow Christ, you are making a serious commitment—so don't underestimate it.

This portion of the book provides observations to consider if you're prepped and ready to show up on race day.

It's getting real.

OBSERVATION #12

Pick Up Your Race Packet

You pay good money to run a marathon, so you should expect something more than just a finisher's medal, right? You bet—and it's called your race packet!

Your race packet is a goodie bag that you pick up before or on race day. The most essential item in the race packet is your bib—the running number you pin to the front of your shirt. If your marathon is timed, the bib may have an integrated transponder that's read by special mats you cross during the race (most importantly at the start and finish lines). Sometimes your bib includes your name, which makes it easier (and more fun) for spectators to cheer for you personally.

Your race packet usually contains a commemorative shirt printed with the race information and sponsors. Sometimes the packet includes paper copies of race-day instructions and a course map. There may also be flyers about upcoming events and coupons for various goodies. If the race features an equipment/clothing drop-off site, the packet will include instructions and a plastic bag for you to use. Occasionally, race sponsors include samples in your packet, such as energy gels or powdered drink mixes.

I enjoy going through the race packet the night before the race. It's fun to see what the sponsors provide. Often, the contents don't have much value to me, and I end up throwing away some of the items right then and there.

As a Christian, you also have a "race packet."

The most important item is, of course, a personal Bible. You may have received one as a gift, your church may have provided one when you became a member, or you may have bought one yourself. Regardless of how you obtained it, keep it safe—just as you would your marathon race number.

Take the time to explore your Bible; it's OK to highlight passages and write notes in it. Familiarize yourself with the major sections of the Old and New Testaments, such as the parts covering law, history, prophecy, the Gospels, and the Epistles. Studying these sections is not so different from studying the course map in your marathon race packet.

If you've joined a church, attended a special class (such as a membership session), or participated in Christian ministries, your "race packet" may include additional items. These might range from information about your denomination to Bible study guides, church t-shirts, car magnets, or other creative items churches distribute nowadays.

Go through these items like I go through my race packet the night before a race. See what they contain, learn what is offered, and study the course layout. But unlike me, don't throw away what's given—because almost all of it has value.

REFLECTION POINT

All scripture is inspired by God and profitable for teaching, for reproof, for correction, and for training in righteousness, that the man of God may be complete, equipped for every good work.

2 Timothy 3:16-17

In another letter to Timothy (who was serving the church in Ephesus), Paul, who was facing death, provides Timothy with some final guidance. This passage contains what may be considered Paul's best advice. He states that the Scriptures are the inspired Word of God. Not only do they equip you to spread the Word, but they also provide what you need to live in the Word. This is why a personal Bible should be considered the most important item in your spiritual race packet.

Answer the following questions:

1. If you already have a personal Bible, how did you obtain it? If you do not yet have a personal Bible, how do you plan to obtain one?
2. Which translation of the Bible (e.g., King James Version, New International Version, etc.) do you have and/or does your church use? Why this version?
3. What other items are in your spiritual race packet, and why are they relevant?

OBSERVATION #13

Show Up the Morning of the Race

Marathons are usually an early morning affair—and by early, I mean *early!* You are expected to be on-site at least a half-hour before the race. There are good reasons for this, including the weather, parking logistics, last-minute updates, the size of the event, how the starting corrals are organized, how far you need to walk to the staging area, opening remarks by the organizers, and (if the race is on American soil) the singing of the National Anthem.

Other factors may also affect how early you need to wake up on race day. Are you close to the event location, or do you need to drive? Do you plan to eat or drink anything before the race? How much time will you need to stretch or warm up? Does the race site have bathroom facilities, or do you need to take care of business before leaving your home or hotel?

Whatever the case, make sure you show up at the starting line on the morning of the race. Doing so requires some forethought and planning.

In your life as a Christian, you might consider the morning of the race to represent your baptism. There are varied—and sometimes conflicting—ideas and practices regarding baptism. Boiled down, baptism is your outward profession that you believe in Christ and commit to following His example.

Baptism doesn't need to be a public event. I've been baptized twice—once as an infant and once as an adult. My second baptism was private because I didn't feel the need for a public display, and my church provided that option.

If you've already been baptized, think back to what you thought and felt when you received that sacrament. If you haven't been baptized but feel ready to receive the sacrament, talk with your pastor about your church's process. Baptism isn't a simple matter of sprinkling water on your head—it holds much deeper significance.

Once this is done, you're ready for the race to begin. Your best running shoes are laced, your race bib is pinned, and you're standing in the starting corral. Your race is about to start.

REFLECTION POINT

Now when they heard this they were cut to the heart, and said to Peter and the rest of the apostles, "Brethren, what shall we do?" And Peter said to them, "Repent, and be baptized every one of you in the name of Jesus Christ for the forgiveness of your sins; and you shall receive the gift of the Holy Spirit."

Acts 2:37-38

In Acts 2, Peter and the other disciples of Christ were speaking to a gathering of Jews in Jerusalem, explaining that Jesus was indeed the Christ—the long-awaited Messiah. The Jewish leaders, however, had called for His crucifixion, leading to Jesus' horrific death. Upon realizing this, the Jews who repented of their leaders' actions asked how they could atone. Peter's response aligns with Christ's commission to His disciples, as seen at the end of the Gospels of Matthew and Mark.

26.2

Arguably, the key word in this passage is *repent*. Baptism is symbolic, but what truly matters is what's in the heart and mind of the person being baptized. True repentance of past sins and acknowledging Christ as Savior is where the real power of the sacrament lies.

Answer the following questions:

1. What do you think is the importance of baptism by choice?
2. Why do some Christians baptize children at an age when they cannot make the choice themselves?
3. Should baptism be a public display?

OBSERVATION #14

FIND THE RIGHT STARTING CORRAL

"Run your own race." That's what my (then) father-in-law told me at every race we entered together when I asked if he wanted me to run slower so we could stay together. I never pressed the matter with him. We'd been on countless training runs together, so I knew his running style and pace. On race days, he always wanted to run solo. I'm not sure if he felt he'd slow me down or if he simply preferred running races alone. Perhaps it was both.

The starting areas of most races are divided into corrals. Signs indicate where entrants should queue based on their anticipated pace. In my prime, I positioned myself in the 10-minutes-per-mile section. These days, I line up in the 13-minutes-per-mile corral. I consider these middle-of-the-pack paces—not fast enough to win, but not slow enough to finish last.

The first mile of a marathon is always my slowest. The field of runners is so crowded at the start that it's hard to hit my running pace until the group spreads out. Compounding this, some runners queue in the wrong starting corral. As I try to find my stride, I often weave around slower runners—some walking leisurely, not even race-walking.

Race etiquette encourages participants to be mindful of others, but there are always some who disregard this. I make the best of it and accept that my first mile will likely be slower than I'd like.

As a Christian, finding the right starting corral is akin to joining a church rather than simply attending. Once you've found a church that suits your style, the next step is becoming a member. This might involve attending classes or meeting with church leaders. You'll likely learn more about the church's denomination and overall mission. Membership often requires an oath to support the church and uphold its values. It may also provide certain privileges and responsibilities, such as voting on church matters.

While the Bible doesn't explicitly mandate joining a church, it's implied. You can only go so far on your own as an attendee. Membership represents a commitment that ultimately draws you closer to the Lord through your service and support of the church.

- As a church attender, you're running 26.2 miles

alone.

- As a church member, you're running the marathon with like-minded people at your side.

The starting corral can be crowded and noisy, full of unique personalities—but it's the corral that matches your pace. Enjoy the company of your fellow runners.

Reflection Point

"Remember the sabbath day, to keep it holy."

Exodus 20:8

This verse, one of the Ten Commandments, doesn't specifically address church attendance or membership, but it serves as a reminder. On the day you choose to attend church, do so with reverence for the Lord. Church membership isn't like belonging to a country club or social group. While you'll make friends and may even do business with fellow members, the purpose of church attendance and membership is to honor and glorify God.

Reflecting on the church you're a member of (or considering joining), answer the following questions:

1. What do you think are (or should be) the most important aspects of church membership?

2. If you are a church member or attender, does the church have a mission statement or doctrine? If so, how do current members exemplify and uphold it?
3. Does (or should) church membership mandate financial contributions?

OBSERVATION #15

THE FIRST MILE IS ALWAYS THE SLOWEST

Competitive marathoners may disagree with me, but for someone in the middle of the pack, the first mile of a marathon is always the slowest. Congestion, walkers, talkers, spectators, blaring music, narrow roadways, parked cars, and sometimes the sheer spectacle of the event can be incredibly distracting. Your pace slows, and you adjust your stride until the start line is well behind you.

It usually takes me about a mile to settle into my usual tempo and truly start running my race. I accept and expect this, knowing the lag at the start of the race is a temporary situation. That first slow mile isn't going to prompt me to throw up my hands and quit. I'm committed to finishing this marathon.

26.2

Some Christians—especially new Christians—may become frustrated because events don't unfold at the pace they hope for.

- Perhaps they cannot find a Bible study group to join.
- Perhaps the pastor's sermons don't address the topics they want.
- Perhaps the church doesn't sponsor a ministry they feel they can support.
- Perhaps the temptations to return to sinful habits overwhelm the church's message.

Whatever the reason, some Christians experience a slow first mile. This can lead to frustration, demoralization, and inhibited motivation.

If you're a new Christian, recognize that the first mile may take longer than you hoped. Hunker down, find your pace, and finish the marathon. If you're an active Christian, offer support to new members who may be struggling with their first slow mile.

Reflection Point

"Take heed to the path of your feet, then all your ways will be sure."

Proverbs 4:26

This simple proverb, written by Solomon, emphasizes planning and focus. If you set out to accomplish something, stick to the plan, but keep your eye on the path ahead.

We all encounter times when events move more slowly than we'd like. When I experience such stagnant periods, I ask myself whether I'm still in the first mile. Will this initial slowness impact the overall outcome?

Answer the following questions:

1. Has there been a time when you prayed for a sign or signal from God? If so, what was the outcome?

2. If you're a current church member, describe events you were involved with during the first few months. If you're not currently a church member, what would you hope to experience during the first few months of membership?

3. Have you ever felt that a sermon or lesson was left incomplete because it didn't address points you thought should be explained? If so, what did you do about it?

OBSERVATION #16

Count the Mile Markers

At most midsize to large road races today, runners cross large rubber or plastic mats at the start line and finish line. Similar mats are often placed at various intervals during the race, such as the 5K mark, the 10K mark, and the halfway point. These mats contain sensors that read race chips, logging each runner's time as they pass.

Along the route, most races also provide mile markers—usually a sign or, sometimes, a large electronic clock displaying the official race time.

I run with a GPS device to log my miles. However, my device and the race's mile markers don't always align, sometimes differing by a hundred feet or more. While this isn't an issue in the early miles, it can be discouraging in the later miles. My device might indicate I've hit 23

26.2

miles, but the mile marker is nowhere in sight. That's disheartening.

Every marathon entrant must pass the same 26 mile markers before crossing the finish line. Runners treat mile markers differently:

- Some like to count down: *One down, 25.2 to go; 16 down, 10.2 to go...*
- Some break the race into sections, like a series of 5K runs. A marathon is essentially eight 5Ks, with about a mile and a half left over.
- Some focus on reaching the 16-mile mark because, beyond that, the remaining miles are single-digit.
- Some approach the race based on where the water stations are located, aiming to reach the next one.
- Others focus on time, pacing themselves mile by mile.

I approach marathons the way my brother once advised: divide the race into two halves. Consider the first half like climbing a hill. At the halfway point, it's like running down the hill; every step brings you closer to the finish line.

Mile markers also serve as points of reference, for better or worse:

- I caught my second wind around mile 15.
- My right calf cramped at mile 17, and I had to stop to stretch.

- The rain started at mile 12 and didn't stop until mile 17.
- Once I hit mile 24, I knew I had it in the bag!

There are also mile markers throughout your journey as a Christian. Some may be obvious, while others may be difficult to see. Your mile markers are unique to your race. After accepting Christ as your Savior, what mile markers signify your progress? Examples might include:

- Receiving your first communion as a believer
- Joining a Bible study group
- Serving on a ministry or outreach program
- Taking on a leadership role at church
- Participating in a mission trip
- Encouraging friends or family to attend church
- Having your children baptized
- Resisting a temptation you might have fallen into before becoming a believer
- Turning to God during grief, sadness, or despair

You may notice mile markers in your Christian journey regularly, or you might miss them entirely. But they're there, and they remind you that you're running your race well.

Reflection Point

"For everything there is a season, and a time for every matter under heaven."

Ecclesiastes 3:1

The word *Ecclesiastes* translates roughly to "assembly" or "member of an assembly." Tradition attributes the book to King Solomon, often subtitled *The Preacher*, meaning one who addresses a gathering. This verse, made famous by Pete Seeger's song *Turn! Turn! Turn! (To Everything There Is a Season)*, introduces life events (mile markers) that all who follow God will encounter. God's people should look to Him in all seasons, whether happy or sad.

Answer the following questions:

1. How would you approach the 26.2 miles in terms of hitting the mile markers? Why would you take that approach?

2. What mile markers have you experienced in life (as a Christian or otherwise), and did you recognize their significance at the time?
3. In your experience, do people turn to God in both good times and bad?

OBSERVATION #17

Expect the Lonely Stretches

26.2 miles is a long way to run. Not every mile can be interesting.

I ran the Las Vegas Marathon in 2005, which was the first time they closed one side of The Strip to allow marathoners to run past the glamorous and glittery hotels and resorts. Those first few miles were very cool! After The Strip, the race passed through the Fremont Street Experience and by the "old Vegas" hotels. That part was still very exciting!

However, after running through the Fremont Street Experience, I was only six miles into the race. I had to endure 20 miles of backroads, neighborhoods, and long stretches before I saw another glitzy hotel. While there were other runners, water tables, and occasional spectators, the long stretches seemed to go on and on and on.

Every marathon has long stretches. If you run with a partner, you can talk. But if you run alone, it's just you and your thoughts. To keep my mind occupied during the lonely stretches, I look around, even if the environment isn't particularly interesting.

- I read street signs, billboards, and the backs of other runners' shirts.
- I try to recognize other runners I've seen earlier in the race.
- I might engage another runner in a short conversation or offer a few words of encouragement.

The long and lonely stretches cannot be avoided, so it's best to simply expect them. They aren't pleasant and may even turn painful. But you must endure them if you want to cross the finish line.

Life is full of lonely stretches—challenging, dark, or sad times when you feel completely alone, even if you're surrounded by friends and loved ones. People you love pass away. Pets you've cared for years grow old and die. Family and friends move far away. Circumstances beyond your control affect your life personally or professionally. Jobs are lost. Cancer and other illnesses strike you or a loved one. Addictions may take hold of you or someone you care about. Tragedies, terrorism, disasters, and disease plague a troubled and fallen world.

Enduring these stretches in life becomes much more bearable if you are a believer. Even if you feel like God has abandoned you in dark times and you're unsure how life will move forward, do what I do during a marathon: look around. God makes His presence known in unexpected ways—through friends, family, signs and symbols, and sometimes even strangers (perhaps angels in disguise?). They can offer more than just kind words.

God, in all His amazing ways, can and will get you through the lonely stretches.

Reflection Point

Fear not, for I am with you; be not dismayed, for I am your God; I will strengthen you, I will help you, I will uphold you with my victorious right hand.

Isaiah 41:10

Isaiah was an Old Testament prophet, and the book of Isaiah addresses the people of Israel regarding their fates. It is a collection of warnings but also offers hope to those who trust in the Lord. This passage is straightforward: if you have faith in the Lord, He will be with you even during the loneliest stretches of life.

The Bible tells of great men who endured lonely periods of isolation: Moses, Elijah, John the Baptist, and even Jesus. It seems there are times when isolation is necessary.

Answer the following questions:

1. How have you coped with life's lonely stretches? How well does your approach work?
2. How have you helped a friend or family member deal with an isolating incident? How was your assistance received?
3. Are there benefits to spending time alone or in isolation?

OBSERVATION #18

Cliché, But True: Blood, Sweat, and Tears

As a middle-of-the-pack marathoner, I have never breezed through a marathon. Despite the training and preparation, pain is always part of the race. I've endured blisters, cramps, shin splints, and chafing. I've seen runners collapse, dodged vomit, and witnessed people holding each other up as they limped across the finish line. I've seen runners with skinned legs, knees, arms, and elbows from falls. And I've seen tears. When the pain grows intense, I've even shed a few myself.

A popular shirt among runners contains a famous quote attributed to United States Marine Corps (USMC) Lieutenant General Lewis Burwell "Chesty" Puller (1898–1971): "Pain is weakness leaving the body." It's a macho and heartening sentiment, but I believe pain is your body's way of telling you something is wrong. Running 26.2 miles is out of the ordinary for most bodies, so pain should be expected.

When I prepare for a marathon, I draw upon my previous experiences to do all I can to lessen the pain. I wear special socks to reduce blisters. I choose shoes with the best fit and support to avoid cramps and shin splints. I apply an anti-chafing compound to minimize friction from my clothes. I wear a hat with a headband to absorb sweat. These solutions help, but I still feel some pain during the race. My feet blister, my legs ache, my clothes chafe, and I'm soaked in sweat.

Some runners believe the best thing to do is run through the pain. Others insist there's a "runner's high" if you push through, an endorphin rush that blocks pain and brings a sense of well-being. While this may be true for some, I've never experienced it. I've simply come to accept that pain is part of race day. Even so, I continue to run these races.

Life also contains pain—physical, emotional, psychological, and situational. At some point, everyone experiences pain. Sometimes it's expected; other times, it's sudden and overwhelming. God often uses painful experiences to help us grow and become more like His Son. Whatever pain you bear pales compared to what Christ endured on the cross.

If you rely on God to support you through painful episodes and reach a point where you no longer feel the need for His support, take time to glorify and praise Him for getting you through the rough patch.

Another popular runner's shirt reads: "Pain is temporary, pride is forever," meaning that enduring pain is worth the pride of accomplishment (such as finishing the marathon). I can attest to this. And isn't it also true of your Christian marathon?

Reflection Point

Consider him who endured from sinners such hostility against himself, so that you may not grow weary or fainthearted. In your struggle against sin, you have not yet resisted to the point of shedding your blood.

Hebrews 12:3-4

This passage directly refers to running the proverbial race set before all believers, encouraging perseverance despite the pain of sin. Jesus suffered unimaginable agony for us. It is His blood, sweat, and tears that allow us to rise above the pain inflicted by sin.

Answer the following questions:

1. Why does God allow suffering and pain?
2. In what ways have you dealt with the various pains in your life?

3. How might someone's method for dealing with pain impact others (for good or ill)?

Part 4: Finishing the Race

In running, it doesn't matter whether you come in first, in the middle of the pack, or last. You can say, "I have finished." There is a lot of satisfaction in that.

~Fred Lebow, co-founder of the New York City Marathon

Romanian-born Fred Lebow was a Holocaust survivor who eventually made his way to New York City. He fell in love with running after a friend challenged him to run a 1.6-mile loop around the Central Park reservoir. He described running as an "oasis in life" where "one does not cheat or exaggerate."

Lebow helped organize and launch the New York City Marathon in 1970. The inaugural race hosted 127 runners (126 men and one woman), who ran laps around Central Park. Since then, the race has grown to become one of the world's premier marathons, attracting thousands of runners every year.

Isn't that not unlike Christianity? Jesus started His ministry with a handful of men and close acquaintances. He offered a philosophy where each person could maintain a personal relationship with the Lord—an oasis of sorts—where one cannot cheat or exaggerate.

Of the original 127 runners in that first New York City Marathon, only 55 finished the race. In 1976, when the race expanded to pass through all five boroughs of New York City, only 1,549 entrants of the 2,000 starters actually crossed the finish line.

Finishing the race is difficult. Even with proper preparation, physical conditioning, and the right mindset, some runners do not finish a marathon. But at this point, the starting gun has sounded, and you are on your way.

This portion of the book describes elements you may encounter during the race and offers hints that might help you finish strong.

OBSERVATION #19

HITTING THE WALL

A common expression in sports says, "leave it all on the field." This means giving your best effort and holding nothing back. In marathon running, however, this mindset can lead to a serious problem: hitting the wall.

Hitting the wall (also called bonking) happens when you've depleted every bit of energy your body has. While running, your body draws energy from carbohydrates, which are broken down and stored as glycogen in your muscles and liver. It's common practice to eat a carbohydrate-rich meal (such as pasta) the night before a marathon—this is known as carbing-up or carbo-loading.

When all your carbohydrate reserves are gone, your body must switch to an alternative energy source, such as fats and proteins. This switchover—combined with your

26.2

body's inefficiency in processing these new energy sources—throws your body into chaos. You might feel tired, hungry, dizzy, or experience a combination of sensations. That's when you've hit the wall.

Hitting the wall typically happens late in the race, often reported around mile 20. Some marathons provide food (such as candy, bananas, or gel packs) at the later water tables to give your body a boost and help you grind out the last few miles.

I've hit the wall once. During my ninth marathon, somewhere between mile 22 and mile 23, it hit me like a ton of bricks. My legs suddenly stopped working. I didn't feel dizzy or sick—I just couldn't move beyond a slow shuffle. I tried walking but couldn't for several minutes. Eventually, I managed to start a slow (and painful) jog. I increased my pace slightly and forced myself through those final miles. Despite the pain, I didn't quit and finished the race.

I left everything on the field that day.

As a Christian, you may also hit the wall spiritually. You could be fully prepared and doing everything right, but something happens that depletes your spiritual energy and makes you doubt your faith in God. Perhaps tragedy strikes. Maybe you feel God has not made Himself known despite your efforts to honor and glorify Him. Or perhaps the weight of the world's wickedness finally pushes you to a breaking point.

Whatever causes you to bonk, it's OK. Believe it or not, God understands. He's been doubted, cursed at, spit upon, and blamed for every bad thing imaginable. His existence has been questioned by people far smarter than me. He has seen it all and nothing surprises Him.

If you've hit that wall—or know someone who has—treat it the way I handled mile 22. Keep moving forward, no matter how slow or painful. You've come this far for a good reason. Trust your faith in Him, even when He seems absent.

Leave everything on the field. You'll be glad you did.

Reflection Point

"For I will satisfy the weary soul, and every languishing soul I will replenish."

Jeremiah 31:25

Jeremiah was a prophet sent by God to pronounce judgment on Israel for forsaking Him and turning to the false god Baal. The Israelites committed unspeakable acts in service to Baal. Despite the coming judgment, Jeremiah offered hope to the weary and distressed Israelites: even if you've hit that wall and are spiritually depleted, God will lift you up and replenish your soul so you can continue to honor Him.

Reflect on a time in your life when you were most depleted—physically, emotionally, or spiritually—and answer the following questions:

1. How did you get through this time?

2. Do you believe the often-quoted phrase that God will not tempt you beyond what you can resist (often associated with 1 Corinthians 10:13)?
3. Is it possible to spiritually carb-up? How would you go about doing this?

OBSERVATION #20

Music Helps

After returning from a run one morning, I told my wife, CJ, that I intentionally ran that day without music. Although she does not run, she replied, "I can't imagine running without music." Her response summarizes the sentiment that many people have about exercise—and life in general: music helps.

Music, even in its most basic form, provides rhythm and tempo during physical activity. Just ask any Armed Service member who has marched to a cadence.

How did people exercise before the advent of the Sony Walkman? Portable music is arguably the best thing to happen to individual sports since the creation of the tennis shoe.

26.2

Even if you do not use a personal headset, you cannot escape music during an organized marathon. I have heard:

- **The Star-Spangled Banner** (a staple before the race begins)
- Music blasting at the start line
- DJs playing music along the course route
- Spectators playing uplifting music over speakers set up outside their homes
- Local high school ensembles performing their best rendition of the *Rocky* theme
- Runners playing their music out loud without earbuds
- Music blasting at the finish line

A friend once told me that running while listening to music could result in an inconsistent running pace. Yet, when I run without music, I eventually fall into a rhythm of my own—grinding out the miles to a simple cadence of *one-and-two-and-one-and-two*. There is something inherently appealing about hearing a playlist during a run.

Sometimes music helps me maintain a specific pace. Sometimes it pushes me to dig deeper and finish those last few miles. Sometimes it drowns out background noise. And sometimes it simply helps pass the time because running can be monotonous.

Music is a gift from God.

I have never been to a church that did not include music as part of the service. While I consider the entire service an act of worship, some churches specifically designate the music portion as the *worship* segment. Regardless, music is central to almost every type of Christian church.

Styles, of course, vary. Growing up, the churches I attended used traditional hymnals accompanied by a church organ. More recently, the churches I attend rely on a church band, with lyrics projected on screens.

Sometimes church music inspires and glorifies God. Other times, it reflects on our sinfulness and need for redemption. Church songs can be joyful and uplifting or mournful and introspective. Music often complements or reinforces the weekly sermon's message.

Some churches use only traditional hymns, while others embrace contemporary Christian music. Still, others find a balance between the two styles. Whatever the approach, music appears to be a vital element of coming before the Lord.

I cannot sing well, but I always make it a point to sing in church. Music provides a way to praise and worship God. Many songs help me reflect on the salvation He offers. Singing also fosters a sense of belonging to the larger church family—a group of like-minded individuals who gather weekly to worship Him.

In all these ways and more, music helps.

Reflection Point

Let the word of Christ dwell in you richly, teach and admonish one another in all wisdom, and sing psalms and hymns and spiritual songs with thankfulness in your hearts to God.

Colossians 3:16

In this letter of encouragement to the church in Colossae, Paul emphasizes the importance of giving thanks to God, specifically through music and song.

Reflecting on your attitude toward music in worship, answer the following questions:

1. What are your preferences regarding music during a worship service?
2. Do you believe some churches use music more for entertainment, or do you think such an approach can help draw new believers?

3. Do you have one or two church or religious songs that you love above others? What makes those songs special?

OBSERVATION #21

SPECTATORS CAN GIVE YOU A BOOST

I enjoy running alone. I do not like to talk while I run. I do not enter marathons to make new friends, and I certainly do not run to show off or impress anyone.

But I love spectators during a marathon.

People stand along the race route for all sorts of reasons and offer encouragement in many different ways:

- Many spectators are there to cheer on a particular runner. You see them scanning the crowd, maybe holding a sign with a personalized message.

- Some make noise as you pass—applause, cheers, hoots and hollers, horns, or even cowbells (there always seem to be cowbells).

26.2

- Others shout words of inspiration, like, "You're doing great!" or "Way to go!"
- Some spectators hold their hands out, offering high-fives as you run by.

One spectator I will never forget was near the finish line of the Marine Corps Marathon on October 29, 2006, in Washington, D.C. I had trained for months and was aiming to finish in under four hours—a personal record (PR) for me.

As I approached the last incline, I could not see the finish line, but I knew it was close. I had nothing left in the tank and was seriously considering walking the rest of the way. But I feared I might miss my PR. I stopped along the side of the course, placing my hands on my knees and crouching slightly while trying to catch my breath.

Amid the clapping and cheers, I heard a strong voice shout, "Get up, runner!" I glanced around but could not see who it was. Again, the voice yelled, "Get up, runner!" I knew they were talking to me.

Something about those words gave me strength. I straightened up, took a deep breath, and started running again. It still hurt, but I found a decent pace. "There you go! Woo!" were the last words I heard from that anonymous spectator.

A few minutes later, I crossed the finish line and received my medal. I had beaten the four-hour mark by about three minutes.

I will never know who that person was, but their encouragement inspired me in a way I will never forget. They had no idea I was on the verge of missing my goal, but they recognized that I was struggling and did what they could from the sidelines. Their words were exactly what I needed at that moment.

As a Christian, you have spectators watching your race too. Some may be family members or friends who cheer for you as you go. Others may be fellow churchgoers who acknowledge your efforts in ministry or service. And sometimes, you may encounter someone you don't even know who offers encouragement during a difficult time.

Likewise, you can (and should) be a spectator for fellow Christians running their own race. Your encouragement could make all the difference. You don't need to hoot, holler, or hold up a sign. Sometimes, a kind word, a listening ear, or a heartfelt prayer is enough to help someone keep going.

Be mindful of your fellow runners. Yours may be the voice they hear when they need it most.

Get up, runner!

REFLECTION POINT

"But exhort one another every day, as long as it is called 'today,' that none of you may be hardened by the deceitfulness of sin."

Hebrews 3:13

The advice offered in this passage highlights the importance of Christians supporting one another. A church, particularly a local one, is a community of believers united in their focus on God and Christ. Encouraging others in their spiritual journey helps them resist sin and stay on course.

Reflecting on your need and others' need for encouragement in their spiritual lives, answer the following questions:

1. How have other people encouraged you spiritually?

2. How can you encourage others spiritually?
3. Have you ever experienced a "Get up, runner!" moment in your personal or spiritual life?

OBSERVATION #22

Water Stops Can Be Lifesavers

Most marathon course maps provide a list of water table and aid station locations along the route. I incorporate the water stops into my race plan, but I occasionally pass a planned stop without taking hydration. Sometimes the water table is excessively crowded. Sometimes I don't want to interrupt my pace. Other times, I feel fine as I run past, thinking I can make it to the next water stop.

I always make it to the next water table, but it can be a chore to get there. Sometimes doubt enters my mind after passing a water stop. Should I have taken something? How far is it until the next table? Will the next table have a sports drink? Will the later tables run out of water?

Those questions and doubts can pull on you with every stride you take. It can be such a relief to hear someone calling out somewhere ahead of you, "Water to the right, Gatorade to the left!"

Relief is close at hand!

In the Christian marathon, I view Holy Communion as a water stop along my race course.

Growing up, I could never predict when Communion would be offered, other than the most obvious times of Christmas and Easter. Usually, the only indication was seeing the elements prepared in front of the pulpit when I walked into church.

My current church celebrates Communion on the first Sunday of the month. I look forward to it like I look forward to a water stop along the racecourse. If it were provided too frequently, the sacrament might lose its significance. If it were provided less frequently, the sacrament might become an annoyance—one more thing to deal with on a busy Sunday when I have plans after church.

The elements offered in Holy Communion have very specific symbolism: bread represents the body of Christ; wine (or juice) represents the blood of Christ. I do not want to detract from that. However, the next time you receive the sacrament, I encourage you to think of it as a recharge, much like a water stop helps along a racecourse. If you are doing well when you take Communion, treat it as an act of praise and thanksgiving to the Lord. If you are enduring a rough patch in life, reflect on its true meaning and take heart and spiritual nourishment from it.

Relief is close at hand!

Reflection Point

Jesus said to her, "Everyone who drinks of this water will thirst again, but whoever drinks of the water that I shall give him will never thirst; the water that I shall give him will become in him a spring of water welling up to eternal life."

John 4:13-14

This is the famous "Woman at the Well" passage in which Christ introduces the idea of Living Water. Life on Earth cannot exist without water. Who would have thought that the proper combination of two relatively simple elements, hydrogen and oxygen, would enable life to flourish? It truly is a miracle. This passage illustrates our constant need for water in the physical sense, but Jesus assures us that faith in Him provides a literal wellspring that grants eternal life with God.

26.2

Reflecting on this, answer the following questions:

1. What was it like when you were physically the most thirsty you have ever been, and how did you find relief?

2. What was it like when you were the most thirsty emotionally or spiritually, and how (if ever) did you find relief?

3. Do you truly believe in the sacrament of Holy Communion?

OBSERVATION #23

Don't Neglect the Last 0.2 Mile

Crossing the 26-mile mark in a marathon is always a good feeling. That is the last numbered mile you must achieve. The finish line should soon be in sight.

Actually, the finish line is still two-tenths of a mile away. By the numbers, that's about 1,056 feet. If your average racing stride is 48 inches, that means you still have about 264 footfalls remaining until you can claim your finisher's medal. Never discount the final stretch because you don't know how you will feel at the 26-mile mark on race day.

In 5K (3.1 miles) and 10K (6.2 miles) races, I usually increase my pace at the final full mile marker and sprint to the finish line. When I ran such races in the early 2000s with my then father-in-law, I would finish ahead of him and then walk back to the final mile marker to cheer for him. I did this when he ran his first 10K. He waved and signaled a "running strong" gesture as he passed me at the six-mile mark. I walked to the finish line to meet him.

When I found him, he was out of breath like I had never seen, and I was afraid he was going to pass out. When he could finally talk, he told me that he had opened it up (increased his pace) but had forgotten it was an extra 0.2 mile, not the 0.1 mile he was used to with a 5K run. "I couldn't find the finish line," he said.

Never discount the final stretch.

Life always presents opportunities, challenges, and goals. These situations often disrupt the normal flow and routine of your life. Sometimes a situation is so demanding that you must adapt to new patterns, flows, and routines. For example:

- Job-related situations such as projects, promotions, shake-ups, or layoffs
- Family-related matters such as illness, pregnancy, or loss
- Social situations such as unplanned events or involvement in a cause you support
- Personal choices such as hobbies or goals you seek to accomplish
- Church-related matters such as participation in a small group or ministry

As a believer, work to view life's situations and challenges from a Christian perspective. Temper feelings of frustration, anxiety, annoyance, or remorse by remembering your overriding purpose in life, which is to honor, serve, and glorify God.

Consider such situations as if you are passing the 26-mile marker in a marathon. You may be tempted to adjust your pace and pattern to quickly get past the situation and return to your normal routine. However, you risk missing an opportunity to glorify God and possibly reflect His goodness to someone else. Hold true to the pace you have been running up to this point. Approach new situations with a Christian attitude.

If you hold fast to your faith, He will see you to the finish line.

REFLECTION POINT

Let your eyes look directly forward, and your gaze be straight before you. Take heed to the path of your feet, then all your ways will be sure. Do not swerve to the right or to the left; turn your foot away from evil.

Proverbs 4:25-27

In this selection by Solomon, he speaks a simple and obvious truth: watch where you are going and stay on the path. If you stay true to the path you are walking with Christ, keep your head up, and stay focused on your goal, then you will realize what He has promised.

Reflecting on what it takes to stay true to a goal, answer the following questions:

1. Have you or someone you know ever been close to realizing a goal, only to have everything fall apart at the last minute? If so, what happened?

2. When have situations in life forced you to alter your routine?

3. Have you ever approached (or have you witnessed someone approach) a seemingly problematic situation while maintaining a Christian attitude?

OBSERVATION #24

Cross the Finish Line Proudly

Hanging from a pegged shelf in a nook outside CJ's and my bedroom are dozens of lanyards, each with an ornamental token attached, indicating the various races I have completed. These are my finisher medals, each symbolizing a finish line I have crossed, nine of which are from marathons.

For years, I stored these medals in a box on a shelf in a closet, well out of sight. I run for personal satisfaction. I am not a braggart, a show-off, or a boaster. I had no need to display the medals, so I kept them tucked away.

A little over a year after CJ and I got married, I entered the 2023 Palm Beach Marathon with my daughter. That

26.2

was when I finally pulled the box out and showed my finisher medals to CJ. She thought they deserved a place of honor in our home, so she gave me a pegged display shelf that Christmas. The location was a compromise; I did not want the medals prominently displayed, so we agreed on the little nook outside our bedroom, which is usually passed by only us.

But they have not gone unnoticed. Visitors see and ask about them. I downplay their significance, but I recognize that, to some people, the medals are a big deal. These folks recognize the accomplishments and acknowledge that finishing races like that is something they feel they cannot achieve.

As a middle-of-the-pack marathoner, I never thought what I did was a big deal. But crossing that finish line at 26.2 miles is a big deal, after all. I finally acknowledge it with quiet pride.

As a middle-of-the-pack Christian, I avoid being too open about my faith. Except for Sunday mornings, I keep it mostly to myself. I see how the secular world treats Christians, so I choose to keep my faith private. I think a lot of Christians behave this way as well.

When marathoners cross the finish line, they often raise their hands in victorious celebration for what they have just accomplished, despite how tired and pained they are. These victorious finishers proudly and openly let others witness the accomplishment of a demanding challenge.

Writing this book has become a sort of spiritual finish line for me. I am just an average guy who occasionally runs average marathons and considers himself an average

Christian. In these pages, I try to tie those two things together, and I lift my arms proudly, knowing that I am serving the Lord with my actions.

As a Christian, you will cross many finish lines as you move forward in your faith. Raise your arms proudly when you cross them. Let others know what you have been able to accomplish because of your faith in Christ.

REFLECTION POINT

Blessed is the man who endures trial, for when he has stood the test, he will receive the crown of life which God has promised to those who love him.

James 1:12

James, the half-brother of Jesus (the son of Joseph and Mary), wrote this letter to Jewish believers scattered throughout the land at the time. Generally speaking, the book of James offers the very blunt theme of encouragement: live as Jesus taught you to live. This passage reflects that encouragement, especially during trying times.

Reflecting on your accomplishments in life, answer the following questions:

1. What do you consider your biggest secular accomplishment?

2. What do you consider your biggest spiritual accomplishment?

3. Is having pride in accomplishments a bad thing?

Part 5: Beyond the Finish Line

"The person who starts the race is not the same person who finishes the race."

~Anonymous, attributed to a marathon spectator sign

Even if you did literally wake up one day and decide that you wanted to run a marathon, you certainly did not run one immediately. Whenever and however you decided to run the race, now that you have crossed the finish line, you can reflect on your journey and what it took to get to this point.

If you have a finisher's medal hanging around your neck, you have proven your stamina, your endurance, your focus, your resolve, and your determination. You have finished what you started. You, indeed, are not the same person you were when you first made that decision.

26.2

Some marathons are presented as weekend events, hosting various races on Saturday and culminating with the Sunday full marathon. Whether you are at the race by yourself or with friends and family, make the most of the overall event. Don't just head home five minutes after you cross the finish line. You just ran 26.2 miles. Do you really have somewhere else you need to be?

Likewise, in your journey as a Christian, when you reach personal milestones, don't just turn the page and move on to your next task. Take the time to reflect on where you are and what you had to do to arrive at this point. Do you really have something so pressing that you can't take a little time to look inward?

This portion of the book provides some post-race observations and suggestions.

Observation #25

Stick Around for Post-Race Activities

I shivered uncontrollably following my second Walt Disney World Marathon. It was January 2003, and although we were in Florida, the weather was quite cold. Worse, a drizzly rain fell for a good portion of the race, soaking me. The thin mylar blanket they handed out at the finish line did nothing to warm me up. I thought about the dry shirt waiting for me in the car.

All around us was a hodgepodge of post-race activity. Some finishers sat alone in the EPCOT parking lot. Others were laughing and celebrating, while some were crying. Loud music blared from the finish line, and the race announcer called out finishers as they crossed.

26.2

Ignoring everything else, we gathered ourselves up and left. When we got to the car, I donned my dry shirt, turned on the heat, and headed home. That was that.

Sticking around after a race can be a chore. If you feel like I did that day, you just want to leave. Sometimes you have obligations and cannot spend time exploring post-activity events. Maybe you don't like being in a crowd.

More often than not, I stick around to check out post-race activities and vendors. Sometimes sponsors or vendors provide free drinks, samples, or swag (such as t-shirts or bottles). There is always information about running-related matters, ranging from upcoming races to local running groups to charitable activities. There may be activities for kids, and there is typically an award ceremony for the best finishers in various categories.

I have to admit, however, that I often do not stick around after a church service. Unless there is a specific reason or activity to attend, I am usually walking to the parking lot immediately following the Benediction.

There are all sorts of reasons for not sticking around after church. Not everyone is socially oriented or outgoing. Some people find it difficult to relate to others due to age, marital status, having children, shared interests, or similar factors.

But sticking around after church can sometimes lead to interesting results. CJ and I once struck up a conversation with a fellow church member we knew only slightly. We learned that he and I shared a mutual acquaintance who used to be my next-door neighbor. Who knew?

Similarly, we attended a soccer game watch party at church to root for our home team, the Orlando City Lions. We spent an hour talking with a wonderful couple, which led to the remembrance of a shared but forgotten experience. It turned out that CJ and the couple's wife had gone on a double date years ago with CJ's then-boyfriend and his brother. Who knew?

(By the way, the Orlando City Lions lost the game that night.)

So stick around after both a race and church. Who knows what the results may be?

REFLECTION POINT

Rejoice with those who rejoice, weep with those who weep. Live in harmony with one another; do not be haughty, but associate with the lowly; never be conceited.

Romans 12:15-16

The book of Romans is attributed to the Apostle Paul. In Romans, Paul addresses both Jews and Gentiles to build and maintain peaceful relationships among themselves. In this passage, Paul emphasizes the importance of humility while serving in the name of Christ but also calls for supporting those who celebrate and holding close those who mourn.

If you belong to a local church, you are surrounded by others who have made the same decision as you: namely, to follow the teachings of Christ. Sometimes you may not feel like socializing—you have places to go, people to see, and things to do. Consider this passage and recognize the times when fellow church members may need someone to listen to them and interact with them.

Consider your personality type and answer the following questions:

1. How well do you interact with others at church (or at social events in general)?
2. Have you ever recognized someone needing (social) attention? If so, what did you do?
3. How do you see yourself with regard to the passage provided? Do you live in harmony? Do you associate with the lowly? Do you avoid conceit?

Observation #26

Display Your Medal

For years, I stored my race medals in a shoebox tucked away in a closet. I got them out only when I earned a new medal or it was time to pack and move. Only recently have I chosen to display my medals, unobtrusively.

As a middle-of-the-pack marathon runner, I am comfortable simply knowing that I have earned the finisher medal. I'm not one to crow about accomplishments.

As a middle-of-the-pack Christian, I am comfortable in my beliefs. But, like storing my medals in a shoebox, I do not overtly express those beliefs. I consider these middle-of-the-pack choices:

- I do not raise my hands during worship.
- I do not display religious symbols on my car.

- I do not embrace fellow believers and call them "brother" or "sister."
- I never discuss religion at work, even when views contrary to mine are expressed.

That being said, I also do not avoid certain opportunities to make my faith known. I consider these middle-of-the-pack gestures:

- CJ and I display a cross in our living room.
- I bow my head in prayer when dining in public.
- If someone tells me about a bad situation, I tell them I will pray for them.
- If someone asks how my weekend was, I do not mind mentioning that I went to church.

Some churches push an aggressive evangelical agenda. I understand that Christians are called to spread the Word of God, but as a middle-of-the-pack Christian, knocking on doors or standing on a street corner is not my style. I will happily serve on a community outreach project, but I will not hand out leaflets to college kids during Spring Break.

I am not ashamed of saying I am a Christian, but I think there are subtle methods to demonstrate the love of God. Such methods can be highly impactful, even if only to a limited audience.

If you are currently a Christian or if you accept Christ at some point in the future, let others know it, even if it is in an understated manner.

Display your medal.

REFLECTION POINT

I have fought the good fight, I have finished the race, I have kept the faith. Henceforth there is laid up for me the crown of righteousness, which the Lord, the righteous judge, will award to me on that Day, and not only to me but also to all who have loved his appearing.

2 Timothy 4:7-8

Imprisoned and nearing death, the Apostle Paul's only way of conveying instruction and direction to his protégé Timothy was through his writings. In his two letters to Timothy, Paul imparts some final advice. It is Paul's hope that Timothy will continue to spread the Gospel in his stead.

Timothy suffered from a certain amount of fear and hesitation. Although commissioned for ministry, you might consider Timothy something of a middle-of-the-pack

26.2

minister. Knowing this, Paul provides this pep talk, assuring Timothy that the cause is just and true. Paul, who had once been one of the biggest persecutors of early Christians, had no doubts about the truth of the Gospel, even as he approached death. He knew that God would present him with his medal (his crown of righteousness) after crossing the final finish line.

Reflecting on Paul's encouragement to Timothy, answer the following questions:

1. What has been your reaction to others who openly profess their faith?

2. If you are a Christian, how do you choose to display your medal? If you are not yet a Christian, how would you prefer Christians to display their medal?

3. Is it OK to be a middle-of-the-pack Christian?

Afterword

When I first conceived of this book, I wanted to somehow draw 26.2 comparisons between how an average guy views running a marathon and how an average guy lives as a Christian.

Outlining 26 observations did not take too long—less than a week, actually. Expanding them into thoughtful insights for this book took about a year.

But there was still the matter of .2. How was I going to approach that? What could I do to punctuate what I've sought to convey in this book?

I hope this book has helped you reflect on your own life, whether or not you are a Christian and whether or not you agree with my observations.

One thing I probably overstated in this book is that I am just an average guy who runs average marathons and ap-

26.2

proaches his faith as an average Christian. As an average Christian, I often see how truly vile the world is. Christians are constant and easy targets of mockery, derision, and humiliation. Marathons are not easy; neither is being a Christian in today's world.

For my final observation, I want to take you back to the beginning and tell you how I was inspired to run a marathon in the first place. If I had not been inspired to run, I would never have been inspired to write this book, over 20 years after that first painful marathon.

OBSERVATION #26.2

You Don't Know Who You May Inspire

Before I ever thought about running my first 5K (much less my first marathon), I maintained an annual tradition of watching my brother Dwight finish the Orlando Utilities Commission Half-Marathon. Standing along the final stretch of the OUC Half (as it is dubbed by locals), it was exciting to see Dwight approach from a distance, pass me by, and cross the finish line.

I also spent a couple of Sunday mornings "chasing" Dwight along the race route when he ran the Walt Disney World Marathon. I studied the course map and drove to spots where I could intercept him as he ran past. Dwight told me that it sometimes gave him a boost to see me along the route, not knowing when or where I would make an appearance. Runners who maintained a similar pace started recognizing me at my interception points. They would wave at me and say things like, "There's that guy again!" or "Hey, I remember you!" I like to think that my sporadic appearances gave those other runners a boost as well.

Dwight inspired me to start running races. He did not mean to do so; it just happened.

I do not take myself too seriously. I run for personal reasons, never intending to inspire anyone. But inspiration just happens, I suppose.

My then father-in-law saw what I was doing and decided to start running too. He took it far more seriously than I did. He logged distance and time for every run he made (including training runs), and he kept every race bib along with his medals.

My daughter has also taken to running road races. As of this writing, she is training for her second full marathon and sends me updates of her weekend distance runs. For having suffered from asthma as a young girl, she seems to be doing all right. She tells me that I am partly responsible for her getting into running. I didn't mean to. It wasn't my intention.

To many people, a marathon seems to be an impossible undertaking. But who knows? Maybe someone will see my medals hanging in the alcove and something will click. Maybe they will recognize that I am just an average guy who is a middle-of-the-pack marathoner. Maybe they will think, "If a guy like that can do it, maybe I can give it a go, too."

Maybe that's the way it is as a middle-of-the-pack Christian. I have my faith and beliefs, but I do not overtly foist them on others. I just live my life, trying to do right. But in so doing, maybe there comes a time when someone recognizes my faith. Maybe they are at a point in life where they need something they don't know they need.

Maybe something will click, and they will think, "He seems like a decent guy; if that's what being a Christian is like, maybe it's not so bad; maybe I can give it a go, too."

Even in the middle of the pack, you don't know who you may inspire.

Tom's Marathons

#	Date	Race	Location	Net Time
1	January 6, 2002	Walt Disney World Marathon	Orlando, FL	4:41:19
2	January 12, 2003	Walt Disney World Marathon	Orlando, FL	4:04:45
3	October 9, 2005	Chicago Marathon	Chicago, IL	4:27:46
4	December 4, 2005	Las Vegas Marathon	Las Vegas, NV	4:23:24
5	October 29, 2006	Marine Corps Marathon	Washington, D.C.	3:56:35
6	November 2, 2008	City of Oaks Marathon	Raleigh, NC	4:25:50
7	January 11, 2009	Walt Disney World Marathon	Orlando, FL	4:14:37
8	March 20, 2011	Tobacco Road Marathon	Cary, NC	4:23:10
9	December 16, 2012	Mt. Dora Marathon	Mt. Dora, FL	4:54:32
10	TBD	TBD	TBD	TBD

About the Author

A Native Floridian, Tom Brubaker was born in Jacksonville and grew up just north of Orlando with his three brothers. He is a two-time graduate of the University of Central Florida. Although he has worked as an Instructional Designer for a myriad of companies for the past two decades, he is still trying to figure out what he wants to be when he grows up.

Tom has completed nine marathons, including the Walt Disney World Marathon (three times, including one Goofy Challenge), the Chicago Marathon, the Las Vegas Marathon, the Marine Corps Marathon, and several lesser-known events.

From childhood through college, Tom attended Presbyterian and Methodist churches; since then, he has been a member of various Protestant churches and is currently a member of a Presbyterian (PCA) church in Winter Springs, Florida. He has two grown children from his first marriage and lives in Winter Springs with his wife, Carolyn.

www.ingramcontent.com/pod-product-compliance
Lightning Source LLC
Chambersburg PA
CBHW060533100426
42743CB00009B/1514